At the seasia

Written by Gill Munton

Speed Sounds

Consonants   *Ask children to say the sounds.*

f	l	m	n	r	s	v	z	sh	th	ng
ff	ll	mm	nn	rr	ss	ve	zz			**(nk)**
ph	le	mb	kn	wr	se		se			
					ce		s			

b	c	d	g	h	j	p	qu	t	w	x	y	**(ch)**
bb	k	dd	gg		g	pp		tt	wh			tch
	ck				ge							

Each box contains one sound but sometimes more than one grapheme.
*Focus graphemes for this story are **circled**.*

Vowels   *Ask children to say the sounds in and out of order.*

a	e ea	i	o	u	ay (a-e)	ee (ea) y e	igh (i-e) ie i	ow (o-e) o
at	hen	in	on	up	day	see	high	blow

oo (u-e) ue	oo	ar	or oor ore	air are	ir ur er	ou	oy oi
zoo	look	car	for	fair	whirl	shout	boy

Story Green Words

Ask children to read the words first in Fred Talk and then say the word.

read   book   spade   sea   mask   line   kite   lie   shade
close   beach   harm   skin   cream   eat   clean

Ask children to say the syllables and then read the whole word.

sea|side   buck|et   snor|kel   ex|plore   a|dult   sea|hors|es
sea|weed   drift|wood   star|fish   coll|ect   for|get   T-shirt
pic|nic   rubb|ish   lem|on|ade

Ask children to read the root first and then the whole word with the suffix.

game → games   pool → pools   cave → caves
crab → crabs   shell → shells   stone → stones
cone → cones

Vocabulary Check

Discuss the meaning (as used in the non-fiction text) after the children have read the word.

	definition
snorkel	a tube you can breathe through while you swim underwater
arm bands	rings you wear on your arms to stop you from sinking while you learn to swim
seahorses	tiny fish with heads that look a bit like a horse's head
seaweed	plants that grow in the sea
driftwood	old bits of wood carried onto the beach by the sea
T-shirt	a summer top with short sleeves

Red Words

you	water	some	your
does	of	all	ball
some	could	water	watch
two	saw	one	their
there	other	said	want

The seaside is a good place for a holiday or a day out.

Read about the seaside in this book.

Things you can do

You can:

- dig in the sand with a bucket and a spade
- play ball games
- look in rock pools
- swim in the sea
- put on your mask and snorkel and look for fish in the sea

- fish with a rod and line
- explore the caves
- play with a kite
- lie in the shade and read a book.

Things you can see on the beach

You can see:

crabs

shells   seahorses

seaweed   stones   starfish

old bits of pot and glass

driftwood

Collect some of those things in your bucket or net.

Hot sun can harm your skin!

Don't forget your sun cream when you play on the beach!

Put on a sunhat and a T-shirt!

Things you can eat and drink

You can eat:

- a picnic on the beach

- ice cream cones from the ice cream van

- fish and chips from the shop.

You can drink:

- water
- milk shakes
- lemonade.

Keep our beaches clean!

Put all your rubbish in a bag and take it home with you!

It's fun at the seaside!

Questions to talk about

Ask children to TTYP for each question using 'Fastest finger' (FF) or 'Have a think' (HaT).

p.9   (FF)   Why do people go to the seaside?

p.10 (FF)   What do you put on to watch fish in the sea?

p.11 (FF)   What should you wear in the sea if you can't swim yet?

p.13 (HaT) Why is it important to wear a sunhat and a T-shirt at the seaside?

p.14 (FF)   Where can you eat your picnic?

p.15 (HaT) Why is it important to keep our beaches clean?

Questions to read and answer

(Children complete without your help.)

1. What can you do at the beach?

2. What sort of wood do you see on a beach?

3. What can you find on a beach?

4. What can you put on so that the sun will not harm your skin?

5. What would you like to eat and drink at the seaside?